THE
TIME
TRAVELER'S
GUIDE

GREEK
TOWN

This edition first published in MMXVII by
Book House

Distributed by Black Rabbit Books
P.O. Box 3263
Mankato
Minnesota MN 56002

Cataloging-in-Publication Data is available
from the Library of Congress

Printed in the United States
At Corporate Graphics,
North Mankato, Minnesota

9 8 7 6 5 4 3 2 1

978-1-911242-00-0

THE TIME TRAVELER'S GUIDE

GREEK TOWN

Written by **John Malam**
Illustrated by **David Antram**

BOOK HOUSE

CONTENTS

7

INTRODUCTION

The civilization of the ancient Greeks was at its most glorious between about 500 BCE and 300 BCE. It was a time of great discoveries in science, mathematics, and medicine. Many famous politicians, architects, sculptors, philosophers, dramatists, and historians lived back then.

In this book we take you on a tour of a Greek town in about 400 BCE. Its streets are lined with new buildings in the latest styles. Merchants come here to trade, and athletes from all over Greece compete at its festival of games. Pilgrims offer gifts to the gods at the temple. The town's inhabitants have never had it so good. In this time of peace, their town has become a rich and beautiful place.

AROUND THE TOWN

The Sacred Sanctuary
Feeling sick? Then go to the sanctuary on pages 28 and 29, where healers will tell you how you can be cured. You'll need to take a sheep as an offering to the sanctuary god.

The Cemetery
The dead are laid to rest outside the city. Find out more about the cemetery on pages 30 and 31.

Craftworkers' Quarter
Everywhere you go you will see the handiwork of the town's skilled craftspeople. Learn about their trades on pages 18 and 19.

The Town Square
The town center is packed with traders and people holding meetings. Join them on pages 16 and 17.

Games and Festivals
The games are the most exciting event in town. What sports do athletes compete in? Be there with the crowds on pages 24 and 25.

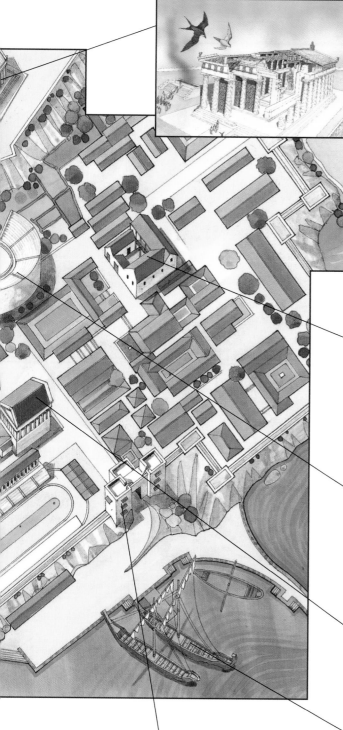

The Temple
Why do people go to the temple on the hill above the town? What do they see inside? What goes on at the altar in the sacred enclosure? Join the faithful on pages 14 and 15.

A Farm in the Country
Farmers in the country grow food to feed the town's population. What crops do they grow? What animals do they keep? Discover the life of a farmer on pages 32 and 33.

A Family Home
What is a typical Greek town house like? On pages 20 and 21 you'll discover what goes on inside the home of an ordinary family.

Open Air Theater
Set in a hollow in the side of a hill, the theater is the place to see comedies, tragedies, and histories. But where should you sit? Be entertained on pages 22 and 23.

The Council House
What issues do the members of the town council discuss inside the council house? Find out about this important public building on pages 12 and 13.

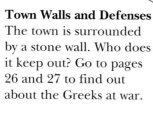

Town Walls and Defenses
The town is surrounded by a stone wall. Who does it keep out? Go to pages 26 and 27 to find out about the Greeks at war.

The Port and Harbor
It is said that the Greeks live around the sea like frogs around a pond. Why is the sea so important? When is it safest to travel by boat? Begin your voyage on pages 34 and 35.

THE COUNCIL HOUSE

The council house is where the town's elected officials hold meetings. It is a public building in the center of town. It has tiers of stone seats which surround a central area so that everyone has a clear view of the speaker. The speaker addresses his audience as if he were an actor.

Up to 500 councilors attend meetings, which are held on most days. They decide how the town and its territory are to be run. Council meetings are often very noisy, and councilors do not always pay attention to what the speaker says. When it is time to vote, the councilors raise their hands to be counted.

THE TEMPLE

On the hill above the town is the temple. It is the home of the sacred spirit who protects the town and watches over its people.

Each town worships its own favorite god or goddess. Athena, the goddess of war, wisdom, and art is worshiped here. Her statue, made from ivory, gold, and wood, stands in the main room of the temple. People can enter the temple, where they may leave gifts of food for the goddess.

Outside is the sacred enclosure, where priests sacrifice animals. Their blood is splashed onto the altar for the goddess to feed upon. Their bones and internal organs are burnt on the altar fire. Then their meat is cooked and eaten.

THE TOWN SQUARE

The town square is a large open area. Traders set up market stalls here. They sell fresh fruit and vegetables grown on their farms.

Around the edge of the square are long, low buildings with open fronts, called **stoas**. These are covered walkways, with stores at the back. There are fountains that supply drinking water from a nearby underground spring. No one has running water at home, so people come to collect it at the fountains.

Sometimes the square is used for a meeting of the Citizens' Assembly. They listen to a speaker, then vote on what he has been saying. At other times, trials are held here.

17

CRAFTWORKERS' QUARTER

Tucked away behind the town square is the craftworkers' quarter, where skilled artists turn clay, stone, ivory, glass, wood, and metal into a variety of objects. Their workshops are filled with the sounds of wood chopping, the tapping of chisels, hammers striking iron, and the roar of fiery furnaces.

The potters' workshop is like a small factory, where groups of men work hard to keep up with the never-ending demand for their wares. Most popular of all are tall vases called **amphorae**, meaning "two-handled." These are used for storing wine, honey, olives, and grapes.

19

A FAMILY HOME

A Greek home turns its back on the town. Its plain white walls have few windows. What lies behind remains private—out of sight from prying eyes.

But go through the entrance gates and you enter an open courtyard, where there is an altar to the god of a household. Rooms surround the courtyard. There is also a storeroom containing supplies of food. Servants prepare food and serve it to the family and their guests in the **andron**, or dining room.

The upper floor is reached by a staircase from the courtyard. Here are bedrooms and a workroom, where women weave cloth on looms.

OPEN AIR THEATER

Most towns have an open air theater. Many, like the one here, occupy an area of flat ground with the seating arranged around a bowl-shaped hollow. This is the ideal shape for a theater. It allows actors' voices to carry to the farthest seats, and everyone in the audience has a clear view of the performance.

The best seats are in the front row. They look like armchairs and are for important people. Other people sit on the tiers of uncomfortable stone seats that rise up behind. Plays are performed in the daytime by actors who speak or sing their parts. They act on a circular area of beaten earth, called the orchestra.

23

AT THE GAMES

When the town holds its festival of games, athletes come from all over Greece to compete in the five-day program of events. The organizers want the festival to be the best there is, so that people will think highly of their town.

The horse track, or **hippodrome**, is a place of great excitement when chariots compete on race days. Crashes are frequent as the chariots round the tight turns at each end of the track.

The race-in-armor, or **hoplitodromos**, is for runners who race wearing helmets and carrying their shields.

A winning athlete is presented with a crown of olive branches and a palm frond. Victory ribbons are tied to his upper arms.

TOWN DEFENSES

A high wall built from large blocks of well-fitting stone surrounds the town. The wall is quite new. In times of trouble in the past, the town's inhabitants took shelter on the hill, or **acropolis**, above the town. But now that the wall has been built the town is a stronger place.

People know that an enemy army will not find it quite so easy to invade their town. The town will be able to withstand a siege, until the enemy is forced to abandon the attack. However, if invaders did take over the town, the first thing they would do is to knock down the wall, its towers, and its gateways.

THE SACRED SANCTUARY

The sanctuary is outside the town. It is visited by the sick. They bring sacrifices to offer Asclepius, the god of healing. This is his special place, where visitors come to seek cures.

First, an attendant washes the body of a pilgrim. Then, the blood of a sheep is spilled at an altar, after which the person sleeps in a cell. They hope to have a dream in which Asclepius visits them.

The next morning, the god's priests interpret the dream to tell the worshiper how he is to be cured. When they leave the sanctuary, visitors place small gifts on an altar, as a "thank you" to the god for curing them.

THE CEMETERY

Burial within the town is forbidden, so the cemetery is on a road outside the town. There is a mixture of different tombs. Simple ones are cut into the rock, others are grand monuments called **mausolea**.

Funerals take place at sunrise. A cart carries the body, head first, to the grave. It is dressed in white, and the face is uncovered. Mourners in black walk behind, men followed by women. The women beat their chests and wail, and one has shaved her head to show she is in mourning. Musicians follow the party.

At the tomb the body is put into a stone coffin, surrounded by food and objects for use in the next life.

A FARM IN THE COUNTRY

Farming is the main activity of the Greek world, and farmers are highly respected because it is their job to feed the people. There are many farms around the town, growing a wide variety of foods to send to market.

Wheat and barley are the main cereals grown, from which bread and cakes are made. Olives and grapes are the main fruit crops, but apples, pears, figs, and pomegranates are also grown. Vegetables include peas, leeks, onions, beans, and lettuces. Sheep, goats, pigs, and cattle are also kept. Crops are grown in small fields.

Many farmers keep hives of bees. The honey collected from the hives is used to sweeten food.

33

THE PORT AND HARBOR

Ships sail into the sheltered harbor from all parts of the Mediterranean. Merchant ships bring goods from the distant lands of Africa and Asia. Some Greek traders even trade with barbarian tribes far to the north, because they bring metals such as tin and lead.

Fishing boats unload the day's catch as noisy seabirds fight for scraps thrown overboard by the fishermen. Some boats bring sponges too, picked from the seabed by divers who can hold their breath for three or four minutes at a time.

Travelers who come by sea only do so when it is calm: the best time is between May and September.

TIME-TRAVELER'S GUIDE

TRAVEL AND CLIMATE

Most travelers come to Greece by sea. Coastal towns and villages have safe harbors where a ship can moor for a few days, or take shelter while a storm passes. If you are sailing at night, look out for lights burning in lighthouses along the shore—they will guide you to safety and warn you away from dangerous rocks.

Pirates are a danger at sea, particularly around the island of Delos, which has become their base. They raid ships and take prisoners to sell in the slave markets of Delos. Donkeys are the main means of transport for travelers on land. Perfectly suited to the rocky landscape, they can carry a visitor and his bags high up into the hills.

The weather in summer is hot and dry, and temperatures reach an average of 78°F (25°C). Winters are often cold and damp, with temperatures rarely higher than 50°F (10°C). Snow falls in the mountains, making it impossible to reach some towns for days on end.

WHAT TO WEAR

Clothes are simple and loose-fitting. They are cool to wear, and comfortable to travel in. Most are made from cream colored undyed wool or linen.

The basic item of clothing for both men and women is the sleeveless tunic. A women's belted tunic, or *peplos*, is worn long. A man wears a shorter tunic, or *chiton*, which is easier to work in. A woolen cloak, the *chlamus*, is worn by men for horse riding. Only men ride horses.

Hats with broad rims, called *petasos*, give protection from

the sun. Open-toed leather sandals worn outdoors are suitable for short walks. Calf-length laced walking boots are best for longer trips. Shoes are not worn inside.

Women keep their hair long and wear ribbons to tie it up, but slaves tend to have short hair. Men keep their hair short and many of them grow beards.

TIME-TRAVELER'S GUIDE

WHAT TO EAT AND DRINK

You will be pleasantly surprised at the wide choice of good food and drink to be had in all parts of Greece.

Breakfast is a light meal of bread dipped in wine. Similar food is eaten for lunch, but with cheese and fruit. The main meal is eaten in the evening. It often consists of fish and vegetables, followed by fruit and honey cakes.

In winter, when fishermen do not venture out to sea every day, a hot barley porridge is the main food eaten. It is thick and extremely filling.

Food is served on pottery or wooden plates and bowls, and is eaten with fingers and spoons. Wine is usually served in shallow cups.

Men may be invited to a symposium—a party which means "drinking together." Women cannot attend. Guests lie on couches and converse about politics while drinking large quantities of wine. After the party, they walk through town in a noisy torchlight procession known as a *komos*.

THE GREEK LANGUAGE

Many dialects are spoken in rural, isolated parts of the country and on its islands. However, this is changing in towns and cities, where local dialects are disappearing in favor of the *koine*, or common language. This version of Greek

will soon be spoken and understood all over the land. These words and phrases may be useful:

Hello/Goodbye:
Chaire (say: khy-re)
Thank You:
Charin Echo (say: khar-in ek-o)
Yes:
Nai (say: ny)
No:
Ouchi (say: ook-hi)
How much?:
Posou (say: poss-oo)
Where?:
Pou (say: poo)
When?:
Pote (say: po-tay)
Have you any food?:
Ti sitou exete (say: tee sit-oo ex-et-ay)

TIME-TRAVELER'S GUIDE

MONEY

Most coins are made of silver or copper. A few are made of gold. Travelers may find the system of Greek coinage confusing, because each town mints its own coins to be spent only in that town. Coins from other towns are not accepted by traders.

Travelers should exchange coins from other towns with a money changer. Look for him in the town square. He will take your "foreign" money, weigh it on small scales and exchange it for the local currency. Greek coins contain a fixed amount of metal, so weighing them shows how much your "foreign" coins are worth in local currency.

The drachma and the obol are common coins. Most people earn about half a drachma a day.

WHERE TO STAY

Greek hospitality is well known so finding a place to stay in town will not be difficult. Some larger town houses have guest rooms where you can stay, in return for a small payment.

Your room will have a chair, a bed, and a chest to store your belongings, but very little else.

FESTIVAL OF GAMES

If your visit is in August or September, you may find the town's five-day festival of games is being staged. The usual program of events is:

DAY 1
opening ceremony
public and private
   sacrifices
boys' running,
wrestling, and boxing
contests

DAY 2
chariot races
horse races
pentathlon (running,
discus, jumping,
javelin, wrestling)
parade of winners
singing of hymns

DAY 3
the main sacrifices
foot races
public banquet

TIME-TRAVELER'S GUIDE

DAY 4
wrestling
boxing
pankration (boxing, kicking and wrestling combined)
race in armor
DAY 5
winners receive their wreaths
closing ceremony
feasting

Don't worry if your visit is at another time, since festivals are held throughout the year.

LOCAL CUSTOMS

Many towns have their own local customs, which can seem strange and a little mysterious.

The main "mystery cult" is the worship of the god Dionysus, the god of wine. His followers believe they can speak directly to him—once they have danced and drunk themselves into a state of excitement known as ekstasis or ecstasy. They may even eat raw meat as part of their frenzy.

Followers say that it feels as if Dionysus actually enters their bodies and takes over their minds.

Followers believe that Dionysus has the power to grant them complete happiness on Earth.

SHOPPING FOR SOUVENIRS

The town square is the best place for souvenirs. Most traders will accept coins. Do remember to use the town's own! Some traders may be willing to barter their goods for some of yours. However, this is now old-fashioned.

Choose your souvenirs with care. Pottery is easily broken if not well wrapped for your return journey. If you do buy a pot, ask the seller to pack plenty of straw around it. Look for an unusual pot such as a wine cooler. Its double walls hold a filling of ice to chill your favorite wine.

TIME-TRAVELER'S GUIDE

Textiles make good souvenirs. Silks from Asia may be too expensive, but locally woven woolens and linens are much cheaper.

If you prefer edible souvenirs, a jar of olives will give you a taste of Greece for many months to come.

STREET ENTERTAINERS

Wherever you travel, you will come across song-stitchers, or *rhapsoidoi*. Town squares are their favorite meeting places, where a crowd of people will quickly gather round to hear their tale.

Take time to stop and listen as a storyteller entertains a crowd with tales about kings and heroes, monsters, and magic. He speaks clearly, raising and lowering his voice in a rhythm that makes his story flow like poetry.

The story will be long, and the crowd will not want the rhapsode to leave any of it out. If he is telling a well-known story, then the crowd will probably know it already. To hold their attention, the bard will add new details as he goes along—he will literally "stitch" the story together in a way that will keep the whole crowd entertained.

Once he has finished, it is good to offer the storyteller a small coin.

DOCTORS AND MEDICINE

If you are taken ill, you will be in safe hands if you visit one of the doctors who is a follower of Hippocrates, the "Father of Medicine." These doctors keep the Hippocratic Oath, vowing never to treat patients for any purpose other than to heal them.

Hippocrates said: "We diagnose sickness by observing habits, diet, age, and work. One should also take

TIME-TRAVELER'S GUIDE

into account sweating, cold, shivering, coughing, sneezing, hiccuping, breathing, belching, and the passing of wind."

After a doctor has made a diagnosis, he will prescribe a cure. This will be medicine made from herbs. Eye complaints can be cured with saffron. Mustard infused in cucumber sauce is used for fits. Severe conditions can be improved by cupping. Heated metal cups are applied to the body to draw off the fluids causing the problem. If this fails, the doctor may resort to bleeding the patient with leeches.

GOOD MANNERS

The Greeks will expect visitors to be on their best behavior while they are in town.

When you greet someone, it is customary to shake their hand and offer a few words of good luck.

If you are asked to a meal, you should accept, as refusal will cause offense to the host. At the meal, show respect for the god of the house by offering a small gift of wine or food at the altar. If the meal is a banquet, expect to

eat it while reclining on a low couch. Do not be surprised if you have to share the couch—it should be big enough for two. The meal may last for several hours, so guests may take short naps between courses.

GUIDED TOURS

TO THE VISITOR...

A new town with a confusing maze of streets can seem a strange place to the visitor. These tours will help you find your way around— follow the suggestions and you will soon feel at home. Greece's ever-popular tourist centers are also described here.

WALK THE WALL

You can walk around the town wall. To walk the entire circuit, start at sunrise and aim to finish before midday, since walking in the afternoon heat can be uncomfortable. In the early morning light you will see fishing boats returning to harbor and the farms dotted across the countryside. After this walk, seek out the pleasant shade of the town square.

TOWN SQUARE

The town square is a good meeting place, since streets lead to it from all directions.

The square is the living heart of the town. It is the

center of social life, business, and politics. It can also be quite rough and the haunt of gossips and pickpockets.

Note the many statues and altars around the square.

You may also witness a meeting of the Citizens' Assembly. Listen to the speaker, then watch as the crowd votes for or against his proposal.

COUNCIL HOUSE

Situated in a corner of the town square is the council house, or *bouleuterion*. A meeting may be in progress. Councillors meet here most days to decide what should be discussed at the next Assembly meeting.

TEMPLE

Leave the square and go past the craftworkers' buildings and on to the main temple. Built on the hill overlooking the town, the temple dominates the surroundings. It can be seen from miles around.

GUIDED TOURS

An imposing gateway that looks like a temple itself, marks the entrance to the **temenos**, or sacred enclosure. As you follow the route to the temple, you will hear the sound of religious music. The air will be thick with the strong smell of burning offerings on the altar fire at the eastern end of the temple.

Inside the temple is the great gold and ivory statue of Athena, to whom the temple is dedicated. Her gaze is fixed on the altar as her priests sacrifice sheep to please her, before tossing their carcasses on the fire to burn.

HARBOR

The cool breeze from the sea will be a welcome relief as you descend from the sticky heat of the hilltop. Follow the main road past the town square on your right, and you will soon come to a gateway in the town wall. Walk through, then on down the hill to the harbor.

Ships bring goods from the Greek colonies of Massilia (*Marseilles, in France*), Neapolis (*better known as Naples, in Italy*), Syracuse (*on Sicily*), Odessos (*Odessa, in Ukraine*), and Naukratis (*Kom Gi'eif, in Egypt*).

Nearby you'll see ships being built— Greek shipwrights are the best, and Greek ships rule the seas.

THEATER

Feel like seeing a play? Then go back along the main road through town and take the last turn right which leads to the **theatrum**, which means "the place for seeing."

The town's theater has recently been rebuilt, replacing creaky old wooden seats with ones of stone.

GUIDED TOURS

Note how the seats are divided into blocks by a horizontal **diazoma**, or walkway, and by **klimakes**, or stairways. Each block is known as a **kerkis**. Every seat allows a clear view of the orchestra, or acting area, behind which is the proscenium. This is a low building with a flat roof which actors use as a raised stage. Their dressing rooms, or **skene**, are behind the stage.

HORSE TRACK

On race days this is the only place to be. The **hippodrome** will be packed with visitors, who come to watch chariots pulled by teams of two or four horses as they race around the track.

The hippodrome is a long rectangular track with rounded ends. Tiers of stone seats now line the sides—spectators used to sit or stand on the grassy banks.

The course is marked by a tall pillar at either end, around which the chariots must turn. The length of one lap is six stades (about ¾ of a mile). As many as forty chariots at a time race twelve times around the track. People bet on the winner. You will do well to remember the saying: "A fool and his money are easily parted."

COUNTRYSIDE

The countryside around town is worth a visit. It belongs to the town and is part of what is known as the city-state. The people who live within the city-state are citizens of the town, enjoying the same rights and privileges as those who live in the town itself.

You will soon discover the many joys of the Greek countryside. The hilly landscape may look barren, but the truth is quite different.

Farmers work long hours tending their small fields, growing food to feed the town's population. They are highly thought of by their fellow citizens. Note their clothes. They wear hats to protect themselves from the sun, short tunics which are easy to move around in, and leather boots to protect their feet.

GUIDED TOURS TO OTHER PLACES

ATHENS

The great city of Athens owes much of its splendor to one man—the statesman and general, Pericles. In 449 BCE, peace was made with the Persians, ending the war between Greece and Persia.To celebrate, Pericles glorified Athens with several wonderful new buildings.

Take the Panathenaic Way, the road from the city center to the acropolis, on which stands a fine group of temples. Upon entering the sacred enclosure you will come before a large bronze statue of Athena, the goddess of the city. To her right is the Parthenon, the grandest temple of all. Marvel at its 46 columns, each almost 33 feet (10 m) tall.

The Erectheum, the most sacred temple on the hill, has columns carved to look like women. Note the pool of salt water in a small hollow, made when Poseidon struck the rock with his trident.

On the other side of the city is the Pnyx, a hill where the Citizens' Assembly meets. Go also to Piraeus, the port, to travel by sea to other parts of Greece. Visitors may go to Mount Olympus from here, to meet the gods.

MOUNT OLYMPUS

Travel to Mount Olympus and you will be in the lap of the Olympian gods, since this is where the twelve gods live:

APHRODITE
goddess of love and beauty

APOLLO
god of truth, music, and healing

ARES
god of war

ARTEMIS
goddess of wild animals

ATHENA
goddess of war, wisdom, and art

DEMETER
goddess of grain and fertility

DIONYSUS
god of wine and vegetation

HERA
goddess of women

HERMES
god of travel, business, and sport

HESTIA
goddess of hearth and home

POSEIDON
god of the sea and earthquakes

ZEUS
god of the weather and king of gods

GLOSSARY

Acropolis Hill at the heart of a Greek town.

Altar Flat-topped block used to make offerings to a god.

Amphora Large two-handled storage pot.

Andron Dining room of a house.

Assembly Gathering of citizens of a city-state.

Barbarian Person from a wild, uncivilized tribe.

Bouleuterion Council house.

Bronze Yellowish metal mixed from copper and tin.

Citizen A free person of a city and its state.

City-state Self-governing city and its land.

Council A town's elected officials.

Councilor Member of the Council.

Dialect A person's accent.

Discus Stone or metal disk thrown by athletes.

Drachma A coin.

Hippodrome Race track for horses and chariots.

Mausolea Large, ornate and expensive tombs.

Obol A coin.

Olympian One of the twelve gods on Mount Olympus.

Orchestra The performing area of a theater.

Rhapsode Storyteller who tells stories in a poetic way.

Sanctuary A holy place.

Siege When an army keeps people trapped in their town.

Stade Unit of length, equal to about 515 feet (35 meters).

Stoa Low building with a row of stores inside.

Symposium Drinking party for men only.

Temenos Sacred enclosure in which stands a temple.

INDEX